Atacama Poems

Atacama Poems

Adrián Arancibia

SD
CWP

SAN DIEGO
CITY WORKS
PRESS

ISBN 978-0-9765801-7-1
Library of Congress Control Number: 2007921272

San Diego City Works Press is a non-profit press, funded by local writers and friends of the arts, committed to the publication of fiction, poetry, creative nonfiction, and art by members of the San Diego City College community and the community at large. For more about San Diego City Works Press please visit our website at www.cityworkspress.org.

San Diego City Works Press is extremely indebted to the American Federation of Teachers, Local 1931, without whose generous contribution and commitment to the arts this book would not be possible.

Cover Design: Reyes Rodriguez
Production Editor: Will Dalrymple

Published in the United States by San Diego City Works Press, California
Printed in the United States of America

contents

foreword

VII
Voz insufrible, diseminada
sal, substituida
ceniza, ramo negro
en cuyo extremo aljófar aparece la luna
ciega, por corredores enlutados de cobre.
¿Qué material, qué cisne hueco
hunde en la arena su desnudo agónico
y endurece su luz líquida y lenta?
¿Qué rayo duro rompe su esmeralda
entre sus piedras indomables hasta
cuajar la sal perdida?
—*(Atacama) Pablo Neruda*

I FIRST MET ADRIÁN at University of California, San Diego in the Fall of 2000 in a seminar dealing with Globalization and Cultural Production in Mexico directed by Professor Max Parra. I later realized that I had seen him before as part of the Taco Shop Poets collective, more precisely in a taco shop in National City some three years before. That night, I was celebrating my final oral presentation for a Latin American Poetry seminar as part of the Masters Program at San Diego State University. Recalling the reading *Entre burrito y cerveza*, I remember being captivated by the powerful images conjured up by these oral poets. It was a notable contrast to my previous presentation on some Argentine poet whose name I have forgotten. Immediately, I was able to relate myself to these oral stories narrating lives of common people in the barrio. Overall, it was a great night, the *negra modelo* was cold, the salsa was hot, the guacamole was real, and the poems were inspiring.

In later conversations with Adrián, I realized we share a common personal background. We were both raised in working class families, we have lived in a desert, we cannot grow a full beard, and we both had an interest for the role of oral history and memory in literature. It is precisely this last aspect that stands out in his book *Atacama Poems*. Indeed, *Atacama Poems* is a receptacle of memory and memory in this book is explored in different levels; the individual level, the collective level, and the "Memorial" (commemorative) level.

On a personal level, this is a story about the search for a father. Not necessarily in the Odyssean tradition, since in this case there is the certainty of his death, but instead a metaphysical search. Adrián Emilio, the author's father, has shared his parent's story (Emilio y Adriana) throughout the years with his children so that they could have a "recuerdo", a memory of their grandparents. However, they were never permitted a chance to meet their grandparents since they died before their grandchildren were born. Adrián Emilio narrates daily life experiences of his childhood and his parents to his sons and begins to build a memory for them. At the same time, the poetic voice is fragmented, allowing other voices to be heard; those of Adriana and Emilio, giving the reader a closer look at the events being narrated. It is through these voices that we learn about the intimate experiences of a marriage trying to survive in the midst of exploitation, poverty, loneliness, and the driest desert in the world. Memory becomes actuality by the use of the present tense in the poetic voice(s). This allows the reader to listen to voices originating in a remote time but that are constantly present in the recollections of their son and now of their grandson. Indeed, the confluence of voices allows us a broader understanding of what is being narrated; a story about love without romantic idealizations, and the origin of a family.

At the collective level, the book explores, albeit indirectly, the life of the *pampinos*. These lives are represented by the experience of Emilio. Emilio is the collective memory of a way of life that faces an extreme climate, poverty, and exploitation in the mines accompanied by a sense of fatalism. Indeed, it is through Emilio's voice, or rather murmur, that we hear the living and working conditions of the miners. In this reading, Emilio leaves behind his individuality and becomes a collective character. It is through him that we learn about the difficulties of getting an education for their children and also about the monopolistic strategies of the foreign companies. Consequently, there is a social angle that is exposed in this level. The work presents subtle commentaries on the social inequalities reminiscent of another Chilean writer, Baldomero Lillo, and his stories from *Sub-terra*. However, unlike Lillo's stories, the children here manage to escape from the oppression and fatalism of this environment.

At the "memorial" level, this is also a story about a personal or family mythology, not in the modern understanding of the word as something untrue, but almost as a foundational story about a particular family. It is a story that functions as an homage; it evokes memories and people long gone, in that sense the piece functions as a way to commemorate the struggles endured by a family. The stories of these struggles have been passed along, and will continue to do so, from generation to generation through the use of oral stories. The author felt it was time to share those stories by transcribing them into print. However, the book transcends the individual reading of it by narrating a universal story. It is almost like a family album that reminds us of the importance of fulfilling our dreams and remembering those who made it possible for those dreams to come true. Indeed, in the beginning of the poem, the poetic voice tells us how two children are taken to visit the grave of their grandfather. The image is evocative to that of Dante being guided by Virgil into Hell. Only, in this case, the poet is guided by his father into the realm of memory, the cemetery. It all begins here, where it all ends. The father is here to inform his deceased father that he has fulfilled his long desired dream. Indeed, not only has he done so, he has also passed this dream into his children; this dream of learning English as a key to success.

"Del mezzo del camín di nostra vita"

Finally, this book also represents a personal tribute on the part of the author Adrián to his father. For his father and uncle, the journey from Iquique to Chuquicamata represented a rite of passage but also, and more importantly, the confirmation and witnessing of the rebirth of a hero. For a moment, Adrián Emilio felt responsible for their father's devastation. Adrián Emilio and his brother Ramón, learned in that precise moment that their actions had consequences and could hurt other people, "Our hero turned into a pile of shredded rags…At that moment, I would have preferred one thousand beatings to the image in front of my eyes and the realization that we were the cause of so much grief." However, just moments after that incident they witnessed the rebirth of that hero after Coqui tried to ease the pain by informing him of their arrangements to attend the public school:

> At first, relief then contentment and finally, utter happiness. That was my father. That was my hero. That was the father who was willing to sell his soul to the devil so long as his sons got an education. That was the man with resolve, the one who would not let pain or disappointment defeat him.

It was at this moment that they learned they were more to his father than just his sons; they were his dream. For Adrián Emilio, bringing his sons to his own father's grave meant the repayment of a personal debt. Sharing his stories with his sons was a way of communicating the importance of gratitude and of expressing it to those one loves. Adrián Emilio was too shy to do so when his father was alive; that was his personal debt. When he saw his father practicing his English he felt like hugging him: "In those days, i wanted to hug my father with my smile as he practiced his English," instead he preferred to remain quiet. Also, one night when he heard his drunken father enter their room to express to them in English how special they were for him, Adrián Emilio and his brother pretend to be sleeping and not reciprocate their feelings. When his father died, Adrián Emilio shared his tears only with his pillow never showing his true feelings. But now, he takes his sons to their grandparent's grave and for the first time: "yes I saw my father cry." In a culture where *los hombres no lloran* (men don't cry) Adrián Emilio's tears function as a liberating inheritance for his sons and a form of openly expressing his gratitude to his parents. For this reason, this book is also the concretization of a personal debt on the authors' part. It is a way of thanking his father for all of his teachings and for sharing his personal stories and histories. After all, let's not forget, in a way, this is a collective work that rescues oral stories from three generations.

The trip that Adrián Emilio and Ramón make from the mines to Iquique to study, is the inheritance that parents Emilio and Adriana left the two. The trip is celebrated time and again as a step towards permitting the children an opportunity the parents never had. This trip will later be repeated when Adrián Emilio makes an even longer trip from Chile to the United States. This time, his trip includes his sons, Adrián (the author) and Diego (the author's brother) continuing the inheritance left to them by Adriana and Emilio. At a very early age, they leave Chile to find a better future in the United States. Much in the same way that Adrián Emilio takes this trip to Chile to thank his deceased parents for having given him the foundation for the future, Adrián has done the same now, piecing together his father's stories in this book.

José Salvador Ruiz
November 2006

author's preface

This collection of poems and prose is based on my father's life. It features the stories he recounted about his childhood. In many ways, he was the first author of this text. From the time we were children, to the time we were adults, my siblings and I heard most of these stories in one form or another.

Through these re-collections, my brothers and sister and I, learned early on the importance of reading and writing. We learned the power of 'alfabetismo' as my father calls it. His stories usually related how his father, a man who could hardly read knew the importance of education and of learning to read. This was so much the case that my abuelo, a man of very modest means, managed to send his children to a boarding school to learn.

It wasn't until I'd reached adulthood that I realized the importance of these tales. I remember the day I decided to write these poems. It was a Saturday in 1992. While speaking to my mother that morning, I had managed to ask what they had done the night before. She plaintively told me that I ought to spend more time listening to my father. As I quizzically looked at her and asked why, she explained. The day before, in tears, my father had explained to her how much he wished he could conjure up his father's spirit. He only wanted to see him once to thank him, to explain to him how he'd raised his children to go to college, to show him the fruits of his lessons.

This text then, offers some of these oral histories of a generation of pampinos (the people who lived on the high plains of the Atacama Desert). This piece is an homenaje (an homage) to my father's parents

Adriana and Emilio Arancibia. They met in the driest desert on earth, the Atacama Desert in Chile. In that desert, their love endured nearly two decades. Miraculously, some say, it bloomed like a desert flower without any water. Two generations later, these stories speak to us about the hardship of their lives. They describe the oppressive beauty and sadness of life's struggles in the desert.

This text also includes a version of a tale that my father wrote. In the ten years since this piece was first written, I have managed to convince him of the importance of writing down these histories. So, in an attempt to capture the intra-generational quality of this text, I have included a piece by him so readers can better understand how such dialogues occur and result in texts such as this.

prólogo

-papi where are we going?
my brother echoes
-papi where
hair plastered
still moist
streaking cross forehead
huffing my sand covered
shoes choke
-¿papá adónde vamos?
-¿papá adónde

-ya estamos cerca pesados
van a ver donde vamos.
-y ya you'll see, be patient

the smell of desert and gasoline
wafting
through my body
smell ripples,
again,
diego & i hold hands
feel his
beginning to sweat

-aquí estamos niños
¿what is this place pápi?
-éste es…
he paused to look to see
if they
-this is the place your grandparents were buried
-but abuelito's not dead

we saw him this morning
-no… my parents

stepping closer
we approach
gates locked
no entrance
papá frustrado looks ahead
under his breath
i hear him say
-i've come

toda esta distancia
-papá te he traído a mis hijos
tus nietos
a verte
a conocerte
y cómo que no nos va dejar entrar

clambering iron
loosens and
                        falls
white head steps forward
pink outline eyes
                                    albino
burning question
                                    -¿sí. qué quieren ustedes?
papá replies
-he viajado desde los estados unidos
          con mis hijos pa' ver a mi 'apá.
          queremos entrar, por favor señor.

-¿dice usted que su padre está aquí?
-sí

-pues entren,
                            pero sólo por treinta minutos
-ya, adrián, dieguito....

introducción

you,
here to see
what this land
is all about
a land, running to hide itself
under mountains
or seas
a needle country

esta *tierra* se ha puesto
the darkness of a land of too much sunlight
dust blinding us
air set deep in lungs
    choking
    constricting hearts.
    squeezing out souls
    leaving it
    dripping like an echo
        crossing canyons and ridges
        of *this desert*
never known to cry;

now waiting for you.

desierto

falls between my fingers
dripping powder
a string
        papered horizontal
        land below
eyes swollen by sun,
glowing a radiated, hot
shoe cupped feet
  burn

reaching fingertips quiver. rub,
desert's back.
stare long enough,
you cough &
  break the silence
between baked earth
  and breath

unturned & outstretched

forgetting names as it
forgets dust
rolling off it

desert leaves.
throats choke
as if to scrape
it-self off
the dryness of air,
an eraser rubbing at moist
births of words

what were holes in the ground
where hands became rough & salty &
        machines dwarfed man
        land opened her body
        to their consuming breaths

bit by bit,
hands
becoming harder
reaching deeper
past soft exteriors
to centered ores
plug &
drive in
plugging &
driving into
surfaces broken with
hurried blasts of dynamite

still,
many
sit in wait
driving fingers through
inner veins
tearing off pieces
of covering behind
reaching past inner lips
taking what they can

scraps always
left for someone else

look at them
try & remember
names
the deep eyes
scraped out by wind
the too burnt skin
exposed too long
to desert
        drying out lives
loves abandoned
empty wells
in the summertime

the towns forgotten
memories
once created in mind &
never thought to check back
& see if really true
&
one day
upon passing,
                by chance,
step on a reminder
realize it never was, it was
instead a dream

hornos
where you made *ese caldo* or
prepared "*onces*"-
                    teatime
as we played on the sand

then, the
oven-centered
our house
of wood & zinc roofs
wind seeping in with a
crawl to our knees
in beds &
after showers
where streams ran from
tank bellies
like ice &
shudder
thinking of skin
only oven coal fires
kept us warm
  in the mornings &
          late at night

hold hands to it then
rub ears neck & face
try & make them warm

like wood hands splintered

crack

break apart sun

wires become edges
of fingers
standing
like
hair,

hands burned to orange afterglow
palms worked to white

lost teeth gaps
glow black
in arching sun
cool spaces of shade
spread behind lips
gasping to breathe
like tar gum chewed
by dry mouths

hammers crack
far far back
rumbling engines pass ahead
grey shirts move a blacker shade, dripping
to sulphur soil as it simmers
tasting drops

mid-day breezes come
streams of empty breaths
blown after long nights smelling of
wine & whores

soles become reminders of hate
slave work built on shoulders too narrow to break
cornered mouths back hope into lost nights.

padres

lying in bed, emilio thought,

y que me importará si ella ve
crist oo cairs f che sees
f i take cair u em bof

por qué tengo que importarme con esta secrecidad
wy bodder wif dis secrecee
dare all, all ov dem r *lunas,*
munes dat i fin' n the emteeness ov da nite
an f da stars tri ta take em frum me
i take nites lon blak hare
an choke rivals fer duh sweet breths
che leves me drounin n
duh sweet breths
che leves me drounin n.
yea dat woman
duh woman i foun on duh san
wi' duh moon cryin
lyin n duh bkgroun wachin us,

f it semes lik i lak dcincy
it dat its all dride owt
in dis goddam desert lan.
its gon dri lik mi skin
dat at times cries owt ov duh moyst curresses
ov dat mune at nite.

he thought of his sons. feeling a tear crawl down one eye. he wasn't quite sure why it fell.

...and down the hill the bus rumbled, shaking as it shifted gears. calluses felt like beads held in hands. all he could do was think of his sons in the english school's play. these americans were wise he admitted to himself; stealing our gold and giving us jobs in exchange. the view of the ocean creased his greasy brow, he thought his wrinkled clothes made him look like a peasant. he hadn't felt so small since he was a child. the smell of the chickens was easing off. as was his sweat. sea breezes dominated. even the widow's black clothes couldn't bring his day down. soon, he'd see his sons in the play. but first, he'd go to the ocean and reflect...

(run)
to the sea
suck in salt air
crushing over flakes in your nose
wet gusts
creasing plastered hair with lemon juice
starched over shirts
burnt by onion smells
  midday sweat
miner shoes glowing red yellow
ask to be shaken
ask to feel the moistness
 of foggy seaside nights
hands burnt over
hands molded into shapes from
              working metal
              patiently
              incessantly

finding the cracks too numerous
spray flies
waking shadows

gulls bow & pick
in the sand

even his
blank eyes burn
like reflections
of the sea

taking worn shoes
in thick hands
carefully ripping
worn rubber off
fingers
threading wire needles
taking the new
rubber soles
cut from tires
sewing
them
onto
leather
uppers
finishing a pair
of brand new shoes

touching his belly
scars
were trails through which
her hands trace
his vulnerability
he turns,
ashamed &
perhaps

turned &
couldn't even look at her eyes

each inch of welted skin
bending into the darkness
and out of her eyes
                                        hand

knowing better than to follow
                                                        anymore.

instead
cu
    cú
        ru
            into ears
lying
in the dark
reminding him
she was there
to love him
to let him forget

emilio te quiero

ella decía
sus ojos ya llegando
a lágrimas
sobre la cara
bajo la oscuridad un llanto de luna
pensando otra vez más

emilio te quiero

the thick dress she wore
cried off knees
kept the ground moist
under her shadow
hands became paws
working themselves
over stoves

esa masa de pelo,
hair bending
from her head
& pouring itself
down her neck

shoulders rounded like
widened hips
still shaking from childbirth
hablando con esa voz
        a tin can rolling down the street

guiding
daughters
moons in orbit
rushing
to prepare food
for the boys
coming home
                from school

¿emilio dónde vás?

what does it matter to you?

¿como qué te importa? yo crié a tus hijos…

so what? wanna raise me too mamá?…muévete ya me voy.

emilio quédate, termina esto….

…ya déjame.

puta madre

emilio qué
da
te

y así fue
como las arrugas ahogaron
a mi madre

each wrinkle piling &
stacking on
waves crashing,
desintegrating
over face and body

soon it was too much

at forty,
a fraction
of the *mujer*
she once was

and how do I feel,

¿qué son hombres?
cosas cotidianas que nunca entiendo
lágrimas,
pequeños pensamientos
que caen de mis ojos

following him.
he is the storm.
i, the sunshine that follows

y mi vida un llanto
incesante como
los gritos del oceano
sus uñas son
olas que se quebran
como los arcos de mi alma

his fury is something,
somewhere, between
locura y dirección

mamá
cuando me llevabas
como muñeca en tus brazos
alzabas tu pecho
acercándolo a mi hocico
nunca me dijiste
que tan dulce es el abrazo
del hijo

y como, en noches frías,
tan tiernos son los pies
del hombre, son como arena,
tibidos y duros

sus hombros, montes
y mis pechos
la nieve que los cubre

tan cansada
y cuando
her man left for a nite of drinks,
she knew he'd spend
the emptiness of the night
in the cracks and crevices of
another world

driving
his hands
into soft earth
holding it
touching it
just as she had been
                                        once
                                                long ago

                                                                                    "*imagínate*"

she'd say to herself
but knew
it was okay to feel
this way
he'd be back
in the morning

longing for his rough caresses
on her
hair,
                                                            aquí,
                                                                    porqué no
                                                                                    aquí

and feel him, all of him
exploring her
falling
to fall into
  caves and pits
& remember
lose himself in her again

pero no,
como puede,
how could he ever want
this *morena* skin of mine
again

& as the night's
stars began pressing
on her eyelids
hands
felt the wounds
man left on her body
scars of opened flesh
burned so raw
the wind tickled away
freed pieces

taking her hand
pressing it over
like a *camanchaca* wind
she covered & cooled
the opening

Iiiiiindia, i call chu dat in a luveeng tone, yur *empanada* feet i fownd so beyoutifull onez. dat moon ov hur fase reddend by duh sun. an i carreed you owt ov duh arms ov yo mudderr like a grabeyard tief, takn hur most preshus ting. hur jool takn as che dide. an dose ferst nites, chu wud ly der, cryin fer duh arms ov yur mudder. i felt so sory i'd wok uhwey an smoke a sigeret owtside duh shack we libbed n. no whore eber med me feel dis durty, dis evul. not eben duh ferst timers. duh childen came like duh nue moon. an yur hart hardind, an i wuz lost sumwer beehind der tiney hans n yur brest. *y mira como estoy hablando*, sownding como uh fucking *maricón*. but i tell jou, adriana, f sumwer beehind all mi misteaks, mi horings, my lubbers, i hid duh luv chu gabe me; the lub ov my ferst two boys...*imaginate lo que* dey'll do wen der older, skool like duh fucking *gringos*, en dey see *como* we heng to dare dollares...pick true roks, gibbing dem gold......*imaginate*

i herd yur test was tursday,
so i kem down here to rite…sine… matricular
deez to boyz.
                    deez to boyz
r gowing to tek duh test
so dey can go to skool
an lern
english frum duh gringos
i werk wid
i no dey'll pass duh test
i no.
how?
bcuz dey r duh best i hab.

pressed and starched, his only suit made the trip into town at the appointed time. earlier in the morning he had woken his sons, made sure they'd taken showers in the ice cold water, and dressed them for their test.

¿política?

pura madre
pórque we wud all
bote for duh persun
who gabe us duh most
bier on boting days
n dat wud be one ov duh best
days ov duh year
because we wud
make a party of it all

a scware metro ov bier
to drink
made us porget de mierda
we libbed in &
what was I gonna say?
dat if i boted fer somebotty else
tings wud reely change?

sometimes
lying next to him,
looking at his back
his *lunares* seemed so black
little holes in his skin

thinking her life just like
one of those little holes
a star in the middle of his back &
how much she loved
his rough brown skin
burned by sun

y esos *lunares* son como
ciudades enteras
sobre mi alma
huecos interminables
que ahogan a mi vida
mis manos nunca alcanzan
mis tratadas de conectarlos y
aterrizo mi mejilla
contra la constelación
de su espalda
y olorosándola
quiero ahogarme
con su aroma
de piel húmeda en la noche
hundirme
hasta las rodillas
en la fragancia de su sudor

the sun
bastard-like
reminded him of choking dust
sun falling across the sides of faces
to light even commas
looking past horizons,
his face a
condor
ready to stretch out into flight
prey
on the slightest weakness
there
in salt & sand
each guiño
could cut into the soft
patches of earth
taking prey
in hands
sweat pasting hair back

smile the
unthinkable

coughed
before beginnings of words
or even the thought of words
tomas el vino
trágalo &
smell the earth
while bread rumbles across town
tells us what time it is
never thinking of a home
secured in your mouth
desert burying us all in thoughts
feeling knots of earth
in patches of hair
sweat netted
dripping across brown-black backs

as another hand reaches into a pocket
and finishes a friday *encendido*

hijo escúchame
un viejo una vez me dijo
el trago
es la única sonrisa
when you've forgotten
pains of lonely nights
cutting into jaws or noses by
talking to remember

pa' nosotros,
viernes y sábados
fueron otra excusa
pa' tomar
pa' agarrarse
un litro y tomar hasta que
estuvieras pidiendo leche

y la sofocante queja
de un cigarrillo fumado
en la sombra del patio
con amigos tan curados como uno mismo

fíjese como llegamos
a ser tan viejos
día siguiendo día
día a día
apagando nuestras vidas
y en darnos cuenta
de esto nos preguntamos
¿qué más hay
que pensar de los hijos?
y las esperanzas que ellos llevan cada día
cada día un párpado

pensar ¿qué fue ayer?
sólo una hoja,
un papel,
una piedra,
un trago,
una foto amarillenta.
        años que van amarillando la piel
        y las memorias de ayer

hijos

WHEN TIMES GOT ROUGH, papá walked straight out of the house. took his heavy hands and left us at home. in tears of desperation, mamá would wire money from a distant uncle, made less distant by her story and long ago memories of smooth smiles. who, in replying would send us *escudos* pressed onto coins and flying paper; inviting us over to his home next to the sea.

and so my mother would trek with us in hand to the station.
leaving us to wait until the bus came.
leaving us with pocket change to buy a meal.
leaving us crying, to go to a sister's home.
her dark eyes dripping off her lonely face,
boxed feet shuffling slower than
black hair whipped by *altiplano* wind.

'cause when times got rough.
papá didn't wanna deal with shit,
didn't wanna hear it from nobody.
he just wanted to lie in bed, listen, and think.

koki, know what's goin' on? ¿qué pasa? ¿dónde vamos?

pin no te preocupes

how'm i not gonna worry, sittin out here in this fucking cold…the bus better come, and did you see como 'ama left cryin'

pin te dije que no sé nada, solo mencionó algo de un tío…trates de abrigarte.

i am…when's the bus gonna get here? we're both fucking freezing. *cagándonos de frío* in these jackets. an we're headed to an uncle's we don' even know.

oye huevón que soy egoísta. trata de pensar de amá por un rato. don't be so selfish…shit

yeah…but i can't…

looking for lights
to crawl closer
& stop

two huddled bodies
nestled in coats
holding bottles
of boiling soup
between legs kept warm

the wind
rises from hills,
then falls
thoughts unsettled
with its whispers
burns hands with cold
make you think of that pain

turn again
look for lights
never coming

wind
sweeps by,
a voice
far back
calls your name
rolls on laps of
mountains
sliding up them like coins
before breaking into pieces

in the distance
where two eyes pick
through edges of darkness

as cold takes away feeling
stand up
reach from
the bottle
of warmth
touch your nose
make it wet

el viaje

It was a trip we feared taking. The school year was over and we were going back home to Chuquicamata to spend our summer vacation. In our first year as regular students at the Iquique English College (a three year high school), my older brother and I had failed to be promoted from sixth to seventh grade and now we would have to face, among other things, the wrath and disappointment of our father.

In those years (1957), the transportation of the boarding students, called "internos," from Iquique to Chuquicamata and vice-versa was done in a bus that was rented for that single purpose by a family, the Garcías, who had two sons as boarding students at the school. The preference and priority in the quotas of seats in the bus belonged to the boarding students, mainly because their parents purchased their tickets ahead of time in Chuquicamata.

These details were critical.

The bus always traveled at full capacity and often many of us had to find other means of travel to get back to our hometowns on holidays or vacations.

The night of the last day of the final exam, was the date when the students were picked up and taken to their families. That same afternoon, the bus driver and his assistant, would come to the school and inform the students if they had their tickets and assign them a seat.

I went early that afternoon with my brother Coqui and waited for the driver to arrive and find out if we had tickets.

Even while doing this, we had conflicting emotions.

We wanted to go back so badly and see our family, yet we knew what awaited us. We hoped to hear that we'd be traveling on the bus, and yet we were fearful of what might happen when we got home. Due to a lack of open seats and money, we found out we would not be making the trip on the bus.

Sad and disappointed, we went back to the house where we stayed with an aunt. There, we waited for instructions from our father back home.

Coqui, always a bastion of steadiness in moments of uncertainty, thought aloud, "Don't worry, I know we are going to get back before Christmas!"

A week passed, a messenger from the mines appeared. Our father had sent us some money and a letter with intructions as to how we would travel.

The orders were crystal clear. "Get on the Longino (train) going south. Get off at the Baquedano train station. Wait there for the bus from Antofagasta that will take you to Calama first and then to Chuqui. Dress up warm, because the desert is cold at night."

At 12 and 11, we were already old enough to travel alone and take care of ourselves. As the oldest, Coqui was responsible for everything. I was to offer complete and blind obedience to him.

And that's the way it was.

That following Saturday, we were ready to embark on our odyssey. Each one of us armed with a heavy leather strapped pieces of luggage, an army blanket, a cloth bag made out of flour sacks, each with four sandwiches, four always reliable hard boiled eggs and two bottles of coca-cola filled with tea. We didn't forget the advice of dressing up warm either.

Armed with army boots (a gift from an uncle), flannel underwear and shirts, wool vests, coats and pants and Bolivian "chulos" to cover our heads, we looked like explorers on our way to the South Pole. I laughed with my brother at our aunt's insistence that we dress heavily, Still, the uneasiness and the obvious fear of having to make this trip alone was hard to ignore.

We arrived at the train station at one o'clock in the afternoon to a place that resembled the spectacle at a carnival. Imposing and loud, there were mothers screaming names of children and babies crying. All around us, there were carts taking and bringing pieces of luggage, boxes and packages back and forth. There were men and women securing their belongings, dogs barking. All the frantic comings and goings, last minute well wishes and pieces of advice given to passengers boarding the train.

We got in the line to board the train immediately, although the departure time was at three o'clock. We waited for our aunt while she purchased the tickets for us. Once she got back, she gave each one of us a third class ticket and in the inside pocket of Coqui's coat she put a paper bag with some money. She told him, "That is for the tickets for the bus from Antofagasta."

It was a sad, long and quiet trip.

We didn't seem to find anything to talk about. We would look at each other and then went back at staring at the floor of the train wagon.

Questions and more questions assaulted us.

What if the train didn't stop at Baquedano? What if we fell asleep and missed getting off the train and continued on our way south? What if the bus passed through Baquedano before we got there?

This overwhelming angst and anxiety gripped us almost as if they conspired against our attempts to hide our fears and worries. My brother, half-way understanding the tricks these doubts played in our minds, decided to exercise his role as assertive leader.

He commanded, "All right, Pin! Let's stop thinking about shitty things. Get closer and let's try to get some rest. We'll get to Baquedano, we'll get off the train and we'll get on the bus from Antofagasta to Calama and Chuqui." I'm not sure if it was the words he said or the way he said them, but they had a soothing effect.

I was thankful for the young man that my brother had become.

At sunset, we decided to eat our first meal. We were now in the open desert called the Pampa. As we reached for the food that our aunt had prepared for us, we discovered two pairs of woolen socks. Attached to them with a safety pin was a paper that read "Gloves".

We laughed. Our tía had had her way with things.

We each ate a sandwich, a hard boiled egg and shared one bottle of tea. The tea was cold but it tasted great. It comforted our fallen spirits. We saved the rest of the food for our next meal in Baquedano.

To us, the train appeared to be moving slowly.

The train's constant and monotonous rolling began making us drowsy. Our bodies began feeling that infamous desert cold. We got even closer, but that damned cold and the noise of the rail against the track, that "raaac...... raaac," was like a drug taking us to a sleep we tried to avoid. And yet that sleep was so inviting. We didn't want to fall asleep and tried hard to stay alert, but we couldn't even look at the hills as a distraction anymore; the darkness of the night covered everything.

Sleep finally won out and we fell asleep.

The cries of "Baquedano! Baquedano!" woke us abruptly and for a moment panic paralyzed us. Almost immediately, Coqui reacted, "O.K. Pin, grab your piece of luggage and the bag of food, I'll take mine and the blanket and don't worry. We are almost half way home."

The porter told us, "It's 4 o'clock in the morning...and at about 5:30 the station supervisor will arrive. Around 6:00 the bus from Antofagasta to Calama should show up...Get as close to the station door as you can and bundle up because it's cold, very cold, especially at this time in the morning. Be very careful."

Wary, and in a cold that went through our clothes down to the deepest corner of our beings, we got off the train in Baquedano. What worried us most was the discovery that we were the only passengers disembarking.

Once more we were tested by the desolate and ghostly look of the stop. The station building consisted of two corrugated zinc steel sheet rooms lit by a sad bulb that could barely shed light on the door of the building.

Dragging our luggage, we walked to the door. Already wearing and thankful for the "gloves" that our aunt had sneaked in the food bag, we remembered the advice of the train porter. We built a makeshift barrier with our two pieces of luggage to lessen the desert wind piercing our clothes and bones. The wind felt as if it was freezing our souls.

That usher was right. I had not been that cold before or since in my life.

With teary eyes and almost frozen runny noses, we got closer, hugged each other and covered ourselves with the army blanket. Resembling a pile of rags, I lamented to my brother, "Coqui, we are going to die in this cold." To which he replied, "No little brother. This cold could make us shit in our pants, but we are not going to die. Let's stay close and try to keep warm. Soon it will be dawn." I thought aloud, "It just that I don't know what's best now, to die or be this cold."

Sure enough, at about 5:30, the supervisor showed up with a lady we later found out was his wife. She sold sandwiches and hot fig coffee in soda bottles. Happy but with caution, we jumped to our feet. It was good to see other human beings in the middle of so much emptiness and abandonment.

They were surprised to find us there by ourselves. "Kind of cold, isn't it?", was the supervisor first wry but still cordial comment. "Come on in, and sit down while I turn on the heater," he added, opening the door to the building.

"You poor boys, you're almost frozen," said his wife, "here, take this." Offering us a couple of bottles of coffee she continued, "it'll warm you up."

"Thank you ma'am, but how much is it going to be?" Coqui asked.

"Don't worry about it son. I know that one day you'll be able to pay back," the lady replied.

We practically devoured the feast of coffee, sandwiches and hardboiled eggs we'd saved as our next meal. We felt as if our spirits were coming back to our bodies.

Now all we had to do was wait for the bus.

About half an hour later, we saw the bus stop at the station and some passengers got off to use the restrooms and have some coffee. The bus was full and the driver was reluctant to let us on. Fortunately, the station supervisor insisted he take us. Finally, he agreed to let us sit on two wooden crates that the supervisor himself had provided. The best part of this arrangement was that trip came free gratis.

We bade farewell to the good Samaritan couple with hugs, good byes and safe journey wishes. Both Coqui and I felt an immense gratitude towards them. Things really appeared to be improving. Once inside the bus, leaving Baquedano, I finally felt at ease knowing that we were indeed half way home.

I also realized that the other worry was just beginning.

At 10:00 a.m. we arrived in Calama, and after two bus changes, we were finally on the doorsteps of our house, happy but apprehensive.

Our mother cried when she saw us at the door. She hugged us and covered us with kisses. Her sons were home at last. We were also very happy, but could not bear those terrible guilty feelings.

It was not fear that we felt, but awareness of the pain and disappointment we were about to cause our parents.

My brother, so as to free himself from the guilt that was corroding his soul, abruptly stuttered, "We…we failed to be promoted!"

"What…" exclaimed our mother, not asking, but surprised.

"We'll have to do our sixth grade all over again," I repeated.

All of the sudden and for a few seconds, I saw her eyes and face become heavy hearted, but her motherly love and tenderness was above and stronger than whatever adversity or challenge.

"Well, we'll see how we solve that problem later on." she tried to comfort us.

"The one thing you will have to do, though, is tell your father as soon as he gets home, the whole truth. You know how demanding he is and how he likes to be told of a problem immediately. One way or another, things will work out."

The dreaded hour came and our father walked into the house and smiling hugged us and caressed our heads. Before he could say a word, Coqui, suddenly pulled himself away from our father and sadly mumbled, "We failed to be promoted!" and we both started to cry.

"Are you sure?" he asked, still doubtful of what he was hearing. "Yes, that is what we were told at the school."

"They'll be sending a letter…" was Coqui's reply.

He dropped himself heavily on a chair. His now dulled eyes reflected an infinite sadness. He crumbled. He was devastated. His pride and fighting spirit dwindled at that moment. Our hero turned into a pile of shredded rags.

At that moment, I would have preferred one thousand beatings to the image in front of my eyes and the realization that we were the cause of so much grief.

We were all quiet for a few seconds. Then, he got up and with dragging tired steps he started to go to his bedroom.

It was again Coqui's voice that tried to put a comforting tone to the situation, saying, "But papá, we are going to continue studying. We have already made arrangements and will be admitted at the public high school."

What followed and what we saw next resembled an enraged lion. Turning around, with a terrifying roar, he asked, "Whaaattt? You little shits. You tell me, who's given you permission to decide what school you are going to attend."

His incredulous wrath could not fathom our daring to say this as he continued to let us know the extent of his commitment to his sons' education.

"Get it through your thick heads. You are going to go back to the English College, and you are going to graduate from that school. Not only that, next year you are going to stay at their boarding school, even if in order to do so I may have to sell my soul to the devil."

All of the sudden, it appeared that a small spark of light returned to his eyes and a strange sensation began to be reborn from the deepest corner of my soul.

At first there was relief, then contentment and finally utter happiness. That was my father. That was my hero. That was the father who was willing to sell his soul to the devil so long as his sons got an education. That was the proud man with resolve, the one who would not let pain or disappointment defeat him.

Our father was never a bigger man and human being than when he'd probably felt the smallest.

Four years later, upon his passing away, my family had to move back to Iquique.

Among the things we packed, we found a box with ten records of lessons to learn English, a British grammar book, and a Spanish/English dictionary.

When we asked our mother about the records and books, her reply was, "He dreamed of the day when he would be able to talk to you in English and he was getting ready for that… He wanted to learn English."

pin would explain,
pap's shadow
could scare you enough.
if he walked in angry &
yelling, we knew
better than to open our mouths
he could pick us up
with one hand
and slap us with the other
papá
wasn't the kind of person
you could lie to either
cause he'd scare the truth out of you

on domingos, papá would wake us with smell of chorizo and cigarettes. as the grease swam through the air to our beds, we'd get up and look for mamá standing in front of the stove. papá sat reading, whistling Barrio Latino. picking through the food, our mouths struggled to eat first then talk. sometimes we did it without finishing. getting up from the table, papá would put on a record, and take his place on the couch. as the music would clear the room, papá would recline and his back gave way. the harp music would pick and stroke notes through the rising web of smoke he exhaled. on cue, everyone made sure not to disturb him.

how could papá ever do something like that. how could he take somebody else instead of mamá. es como, cómo could he ever look at another person like he did mamá. and what about that motherfucker claiming papá is his father too, man why does he want to ruin my life, why does he want to ruin our lives, especially after papá died. why's he got to lie like that. lettin other kids think that he is my half brother, when he's nothing but a bastard; a bastard looking for a father. but i know better than the fools that do listen. y ése huevón lalo trying to tell coki who papá slept with. that drunk of a cousin can't even see outside his own bottle. can't believe he's even listening to that bastard. papá couldn't ever do something that bad, that dirty.... how could...

dale un chute ramón……
                                        y
gooooo
            ooooo
                        oooooool!
que maraviiii
                        lla
si
            que maraviiiiilla
ladies and gentlemen
dis is juan ov da most incredible feats
i have ever seen
a goal from a corner kiick
gooooooooooooooooooool
para
            chiiiiiiiiiile
brasíl goes home
                            a looooser
sí
con ese gol gana chile
chile uno
brasil
            zeeeroooooo!
a beautifull
shot ladies an gentlemen.

trapping the ball
ramón
dusts his shoes
turns and goes home
with his brother

by the time we were ten, every year, papá would take us by hand to the station where we would board a bus and go to school. i remember how different my mother would look at us on those days. as ramón and I would walk out, my baby brother cacho would grab our legs crying for us not to go. and because of that, it was hard to not to cry. but papá would take us by our shoulders and guide us out to the street. mamá would tell us to be strong.

we knew every year when it was time for us to leave. see, we could feel the fall wind roll off the mountains with more urgency and how it cut into your legs in the mornings. we also knew when it was time to go, we heard our sister's teeth chatter in the cold of dawn...by then, we both knew the sheets we used during summer had to be returned.

when we left, i always wondered what would happen if my father died while we were away.

returning
to the mountains
meant so many things

mamá would write
for us to come home
so ramón & i
would scrape together
all the change
we had &
bought our sisters candy
small pencils, toys
to play with
&

using the bread bags
we'd fill them all up
with clothes & our presents
& returned on the bus
back to calama
where papá would
ask where we'd been
joking with us like old friends
telling us we shouldn't have
left him and mamá

en el carrete voy a buscar carbón
con el carrete voy a buscar carbón
mi papá sent me
to get some charcoal
he put 25 centavos in mi hand
so i gotta go ....

ramón espérame,
porqué no llevas el carrete

¿porqué ? porque no.

c'mon ramón, take el carrete
so we can go and get the charcoal

te dije que no

man i'm gettin tired and
if ya don't stop i'm going to

ok pin i'll take it,
but next time, don't tell dad you will,
'cause you never make it up this goddamn hill.

children's
hair combed to stay
                                                  wet
smelling of lemon juice or guava seeds
scrubbed ears red
still half asleep
taking time to smell edges
coffee cups
warming hands
shirts pressed the night before gave
no hint
of home

papá roaring each time
either of us
would come close
to staining clothes
'¡no te acerques a la mantequílla!'
'¡careful not to spill!'
'¡brush the migas off your pants!'

so they sat quietly
never understanding his anger

like on a string, papá
took us one day
to the end of town.
you know, in our nicest.
and we rode the bus,
it was one of the few times we rode it
all the way across town
but he told us he did not want us to dirty our
clothes
& told us not to forget the lessons he'd taught us at
home
after stepping off the bus full of grown men
all with the same cologne,
all headed for office work.
papá took us by our hands to a church
where they had a lot of tables spread out.
not a catholic church,
which made us feel even stranger
'cause we rarely even went to *misa.*
after telling us to do our best,
papá took us by the hand to one of the pastors.
we didn't understand what they were talking about
but i heard papá stutter out, 'deez r de best i
hab…lo mejor que tengo'
imagínate how ramón and i felt
…always remember that
cause ramón and i looked at him in the eyes and
smiled.

por qué inglés
que consume nuestra vida
inglés
comida que damos
para comer
lengua para comprender
los ojos de mis hijos
ya están perdidos
y perdiéndome en la lengua
inglés
lengua de piedra
donde se me esconden los hijos
ojos humedecidos
ya se apagan
como velas
vienen y se van
sólo a regresar
corromper
a mis hijos
ese lenguaje
escondiendo
las queridas palabras de mis niños
hasta que no entiendo
y no me siento como la madre
que unos años atrás fuí

and the records would begin…

hello my name is…*diga su nombre*

khellow mye name ees emilio
khellow mye name ees emilio arancibia
hello this is my family
khellow dees ees mye pamily
khellow dees ees mye family
hello these are my…
khellow dees r mye children

día after día my papá would practice his english while my brother smirked, never with bad intent. in those days, i wanted to hug my father with my smile as he practiced his english. and my mother would continue arguing with him.

pagó medio
de su salario
¿pa' comprar qué? '
'discos, tonterías
tonterías'
'dinero
que podríamos haber
usado para comprar
ropa para los niños

now that i'm grown
i think of my feet
vulnerable
white.
back then
my feet were
rough edges
moving mountains
with sweat and persistence
playing,
we shone
sweat scarred bodies
sighing at the sight
of dusk crawling on the backs
of buildings. buildings
later swallowed whole
on the horizon
fingers and feet
were the last things i felt.
bellies.
balls.
backs.
sun at a distance.

one
a soul in the flour of earth
crying to live

take the edges of feet
burn a line
in the hot sand
trace the edge of a cool shadow
let them taste
warmth brewing under the sun
coolness hiding in the night
make them one
on an afternoon
before té
feet scampered home
under parent whistles.
chalked hands
cough across the street
awaiting tables
warmed with bread & tea

after the mountains
circle your life
beg sky for mercy
escape seems
so far away
a breath reminding
heat
the crackling halitosis
of shacks called home
barefoot memories
child…*nadie te dijo*
no one ever told
how the whole
might be swallowed
by long shadows of deserts
brushing over the sky
dust
echo
tears

remember…

he remembered how his father had told him '…we did not get paid in real money for a very long time…because we were always paid weekly in *fichas*…american companies would force us to buy their products at their general stores…those fichas were worthless on the outside…and for a time, our neighborhood seemed like a cell, we couldn't travel, we couldn't get certain things we needed…remember how we could not get you shoes for kindergarten…it wasn't because we didn't get paid enough…its just that the general store didn't have children's shoes and we couldn't go anywhere else and buy those items since they wouldn't take our fichas…'

he remembered how it pained his father to tell him this.

'it was humiliating knowing you had worked your ass off and you couldn't even buy your children shoes..that's why i would not let you and your brother attend school…no way was i going to let you walk around without shoes…that kind of poverty makes me sick…like a poor house lit by a dim lonely light bulb…'

remembering this he would take another swig,

'trabajamos como esclavos, créemelo trabajamos como esclavos de mierda…'

y la espalda marcaba el tiempo con dolor y un color siempre

morado por el sol.

my uncles stayed a distance away from my father. they knew him. respected him. and though they never said this to his face, it was understood. my hulking father was a presence to be feared at home or otherwise. they could never forgive him for leaving their sister and even once threatened to not let him see her. still, they said, he had the *huevos* to move and raised his family in the *montes*. for that he had to be respected…

every now and then though. under their breaths, they would think. who the fuck is this *vago* taking our sister and leaving her like that.
no respect for his woman.
and dumping her on us.
as if we were her parents.
we have enough problems of our own.

when we were supposed to begin schooling. ramón and i did not have any shoes, my father being too embarassed to send us to school without them, decided he would teach us at home. every day when he returned from work we were cleaned and ready at the table; ready to learn. there he sat, a man barely literate himself. but he taught us how to read, add subtract; all at the kitchen table. every day, two hours he would sit us down, little by little learning, teaching us to read.

a - es para analfabeto
que es lo que soy yo…
b - es para el burro que vas a ser
si no vas a la escuela

día trás día

& you know, by the time the following year rolled around, ramón and i enrolled; with shoes. in fact, we read well enough to actually skip a grade.

after coqui & i
graduated from sixth grade
he stumbled into our room
smelling of beer
he woke us in the dark
and began talking to us in english

i no i kant
speek dat well
but i want to tell
you
boys
dat i am prowd
so prowd
running his hands
through our hair

although i was awake
i played asleep
because i didn't know what to say
ramón did the same, see
cause if we had not
i know my jaws would have tightened
and my body would have felt heavy
still my eyes burned. cause
even with them tightly sealed
tears fell silently on my pillow

in boarding school, we could not and did not talk about being poor. that was the most difficult part to swallow about school. *esos huevones siempre andan hablando* talking as if they knew what poor was. poor's when you don't have shit to eat or when you don't have shoes, when you can't afford new socks or a date. and being poor was never accepted then, but when the fools tried to tell you what poor was, it was enough to get your fists tight. worse yet, when i worked, cooking breakfast at school, they would talk to me like a waiter. i felt like i had to fight. and ramón would take me aside and tell me that it didn't mean a thing....
but it did,
didn't
it?

yo veía
que los niños
ya que crecían
se ponían más como hombres
y ya entendían los gringos

finalmente
sabía que los gringos
les respetaban
y por eso
cuando emilio falleció
les dieron
becas a cada uno

me acuerdo
cómo lloraba ramón
cuando le dijeron
lo que había pasado
y después cómo...
cómo se quedaba tan solito en su pieza
pensando como sobreviviríamos

y que él no podría
regresar a escuela
y adriancito
se quedaba tan callado
y aunque él conocía
las lágrimas
siempre las guardaba para la noche

siempre sobre su almohada tan calladito

train hanging off
hill
snapping rail ends
easing into hill
slowly scooting forward
 as
two boys
stuck foreheads out
 looking
outside
the town below
spun thoughts
of early childhood
when memories
are little more than wet swaths
of gray cloth
watered by warm voices

remembering sky
a gray sky
a sea
a gray green sea
where breezes came
vultures above were forgotten
as were unending rocks &
sand

muerte

is death in you?
or is death a nomad, a
pacing shadow
only animals see
whose hand can
settle on a shoulder
                & heard
                tíos
                talking, speaking
                of la muerte y como
                el gallo cantaba en verlo
                while dogs sat
                mouth's hanging
                watching death walk
                quietly across town

& no one
          understood
                                no one
felt death's
          falling carnations
burning sweet as cinnamon
while palms
          made fans of streets
women weeping
walking over
breaking backs of
desert palms, palmas, lines

y el clavel
          a carnation

like a ring
flashes
the only color
worn
        desert
                coughing to blow
                away silk smooth
                edges of claveles carnations
                bowing off jackets &
                vases weeping in the sun
backs blackened
baking

blinds
behind veils
leaving empty shoes on unsturdy legs
bent in the distance

men who cannot cry
let moisture bend
their backs &
eyes without
words to say
mute fear of breaking
                    death down
spreads chalk across faces
whitened.
    burning
pain & fear away
    standing

love fades,
crying to live
tender moments   once again
tears well dry
on the endless sun

shshshshshshsh

y tu muerte
sí tú muerte
sí tú que haces aquí
qué haces aquí
ya ándate
ya ándate
ándate
go, go away
the brujera
would say, but
everyone would say
she was crazy,

never ever paying
any attention

shshshshshshshshshsh

                                        viejo no te olvides
                                                de tu abrigo-

she would say &
slumping, he
would throw on
his jacket
with a shrug
notice
how slowly
he'd begun to walk
                                        his
top heavy shadow stretching
out the doorway in
early mornings
                                y
así entraba
el beso del aire
entraba
air entering
like the moist
touch of a child's runny nose

nunca
no, nunca pensaba
she never ever
would think
how life would be
without him
after so many years
she had grown
        to know his
                smile was hers
                        like a tooth
                                in her mouth

those wide shoulders
would jut out
of her mouth, just
like his name
                        -emilio-
slipping just past lips
just
        between

her
lips

each
bus ride through the middle
of the desert
colors wailing in the distance
graves
no, not graves
but
crosses over women &
men buried under rocks
above ground
another stone
in the desert &
after días sagrados
blinding highlights of
flowers sprinkling
death's mouth
with wilting petals
fading like old eyes

cosidas
cosidas
todas cosidas
all knit
all of them, knit crosses
bearing death's
necessary expense
in tanned land
expanse
while a drunk rides
into desert
smiling,
suicide sweet as
last bottle
cooing his name
in the wind
-nooooooooo-

nothing left &
i'm coming
muerte singing
-i'm coming to be with you-
por qué te fuiste
por qué te fuiste
sí. ¿por qué me dejaste?
so
so
so alone
-we're going to be together
mi hijita-

el hambre
de la inmensa noche
ahogándome
como grano de arena
en el oceano
que es la noche

mira,
estás
más
allá
o
escuchas
el
eco eco
de los pasos
pasos
muertos
rumbando
por los cerros
masticando
al altiplano
moliendo la harina
de la masa humana

usáis tu dedo
marcáis

el horizonte como labio exasperado
y luego entenderás
que el desierto es
una pena siguiente
que en conocerte
aparece como un escalofrío

tratas también de entender
la lágrima lenta cayendo
                                                amor
                                                dolor
                                                muerte
                                                                así sucede la vida
y este desierto
carcome
estos granos de humanidad

she would say

-no entiendo-

everytime el doctor
would explain
there's another complication
waiting for an explanation
but realizing the gravity
she summoned her two boys
from school

clavel
could
smell past shadows
making them lick their lips
while rocks
cried to live
with sun
an orange amber
to no end

the sky
an inverted
pyramid of lies
ready to fall on you
crush you & then,
grumble in the distance

the men
drunk late at night
would raise their cups
among shouts &
remembrances
remember
'member memories
memorias, ¿cuántas más?
¿qué hay más?
¿qué memorias?
memorized expressions
grown men
watered by wine &
tears
porque el compadre
era buen hombre
un hombre dicho
un hombre bueno

i guess
that's most painful to me, the
thoughts, the memory, the
scar of chalk
sweetened by sand &
'membered how
he wouldn't let us stay
up on christmas eve
but would send us to sleep
the pain of what we wouldn't have
                                                  was
                                                      too bitter

christmas never celebrated
others received gifts &
smiles
we went to bed early
with mug of chocolate
to help us forget navidad
but how could i
forget my father's evaporating face
on days such as those

and as much
as my father
mistreated and argued
with my mother
i felt
his love in caresses
after dinner on the couch

collapsing somewhere
i know i will see my father again
taint my blood
bleed to kiss his forehead
& let him know
i too
understood

i think of when he died
but remember more
thoughts of carnations
& crosses spread across the ground
wind tickled
our ears

sitting
feeling think feel
burning
only burning
a match never ending
lit never ending
until flesh decides
to cry & live alone
at edges of body

puta, tengo que levantarme
go back…work
esta úlcera
conche mi madre
maybe if i rub it
it'll go 'way
            -adriana get me my cigarrillos-
por favor señor
acuéstese
tratas de descansar
            -adriana quiero sentir la lluvia
            hija quiero sentir tu pelo…
                        en la lluvia
            -adriana cuídame
                        señor arancibia las píldoras
                        le harán bien
                        no se preocupe

                        pills didn't make him better
                        mi 'ama grabbing
                        blanket edges
                        while trying to soothe
                        his pain
                        with a cucurucucuing voice

-emilio descansas
descansas corazón mío
y cuando te mejores
vamos al sur
vamos a ver el resto del país
sí guaguíta
quédate
tran
qui
lo

when we arrived home
i had to make the fire
the house cooler
because of tears
his huge hulking body
nowhere in sight, the
house seemed half-empty

casi pa' dar susto

la casa
creeping closer,
closer to death
while cachito
sat crying
after seeing papá
lying quiet
girls laying down
without dinner
their stomachs forever empty
ramón holding mom's hand
while she prepared
his funeral
his viewing
his burial
y yo,
yes i would
sit warming my hands
in fire's path

la muerte swallows life

-adriana
          adrianita
                              dónde estás?
¿dónde
                         estás hijita?
vente pa cuidarme
vente   pa
                              cuidarme
el sol me 'stá quemando
                                    hija
el sol me 'stá quemando
mis manos
               ya, ya no las siento

sólo	only
escucho	hear
el múrmuro	murmur
of life	de vida
cruzándo mi corazón	crossing my heart
y los hijos	the children

por favor hija traígamelos
pa'…
          so i…
                    pa' que…

shortly after
my mother passed too
sí, ella falleció
terrible times followed
uncles breaking apart our family
taking my sisters
my brother
while all the things
my father had worked
so hard for
were taken and lost
from our house &
these recuerdos
became the oily memories
we had left
in the used matchbox
of our family's story

epílogo

although he tried walking calmly, he knew he had little time. after grabbing his childrens' hands, he stepped with a quicker set pace. the children saw years fly by them, 1810, 1850, 1870, 1910, 1940, 1960. stop. their eyes settled on a pair of humble graves. graves that were nothing more than plaques with names inscribed. EMILIO ARANCIBIA 1920-1961 and ADRIANA ARANCIBIA 1922-1963. the children could smell the sadness in their father's eyes. he took his hand, slowly wiping the names as if they were extensions of his fingers. quietly he began to speak.

with
knots undone
throats collect dry air
cholguanes-
those zinc roofed spaces
darkness rooted
where wind still
sweeps the backs
        of legs
breaks
focus
where breath lies
rotating time
spins breath

sighing, breathing
        - aquí estoy… perdóname por haberme tardado tanto

eyes watered
he remembers
his father in front of a table
        - les traje esto…
smiles laughing a coughed tear sighing
remembers

        - der de best i hab

i saw
papá talk
slowly at first
                dryness in his voice
burning away phlegm
diego
        holding my hand
would ask,
        ¿ari,
            how come dad's
            talking to dead people?
        ¿they can't hear them,
                    can they?
i touch
        somberness of moment, &
heard papá say
            -y aquí les he traído
        mis hijos
            sus nietos

y la adolorida marcha
de una lágrima
            yes i saw my father cry
            for first time
saw his eyes burn wet as
        he took us & the flowers we'd carried
            to the small plaques on the wall

i held diego's hand tight
to help him not be scared
                    as we lay flowers
                              on graves
nobody
it seemed,
ever laid flowers
                              on.

about the author

Adrián Arancibia is a poet, writer, and educator. He, along with Adolfo Guzmán-López and Miguel-Ángel Soria, founded the seminal Chicano spoken-word collective the Taco Shop Poets in 1994.

Adrián Arancibia was born in Iquique, Chile in 1971. Since 1980, he has resided in San Diego, California. Arancibia is the co-editor of the *Taco Shop Poets Anthology: Chorizo Tonguefire* and currently writes for the *San Diego Union Tribune* and for national magazines like *The Green Magazine*. A founder of the performance artspace, Voz Alta, he is currently completing his Ph.D. in Literature at U.C. San Diego. In 2004, Arancibia became an assistant professor at Miramar Community College. His creative work depicts and comments on the lives of immigrants on the border. His critical work focuses on performance poetry and the genre's relation to social spaces. He thanks his parents, Adrián and Victoria who have sacrificed everything for their children and grandchildren's dreams. He offers gratitude to his brothers, sisters, nieces and nephew who have taught him that a full home and laughter are cures to all ills. With his wife Delia, he has found that elusive step that haunts us all, balance.